WYLAM

A history in photographs of a Tyne Valley village

Selected and annotated by Philip R. B. Brooks

in association with
Wylam Parish Council

First published in 1995 by Northumberland County Library,
The Willows, Morpeth, Northumberland NE61 1TA

Printed by Pattinson and Sons, Newcastle upon Tyne

British Library Cataloguing-in-Publication data

A catalogue record for this book is available from the British Library

ISBN 1 874020 14 0

FRONT COVER
'Puffing Billy' is one of the original Wylam locomotives of 1813 designed by William Hedley, the colliery manager, and built at Wylam with assistance from blacksmith Timothy Hackworth and enginewright Jonathan Forster. It worked on the 5 mile waggonway hauling chaldron waggons between Wylam Colliery and the river staithes at Lemington, where the coal was transferred to keels, for transport to seagoing vessels at the mouth of the Tyne. This photograph (the earliest in this book) was taken at the Haugh Pit in the early 1860s and shows 'Puffing Billy' with the driver J Carr (right) and fireman W Greener (left). In the background are three buildings still standing today — the former school of 1854 (far left), Laburnum House (centre) and the Wesleyan Chapel of 1834 (before extension in 1876) on the extreme right. In 1862 'Puffing Billy' was taken to London for an exhibition associated with the new Patent Office (now Science) Museum, and was subsequently purchased by the Patent Office for £200, — a price which the owner Captain E A Blackett thought quite inadequate!

INTRODUCTION

Wylam is situated on the banks of the River Tyne, midway between Newcastle upon Tyne and Hexham, and two miles south of Hadrian's Wall.

The first references to Wylam occur shortly after the Norman Conquest when the manor of Wylam was in the possession of Tynemouth Priory. It had probably been given to the Priory by Guy de Baliol, Lord of Bywell at about the time of its foundation c. 1085. The Prior subsequently established a house at Wylam where he occasionally held his Manor Court. The records of the Priory are contained in the Tynemouth Cartulary and give various details of the Prior's tenants in Wylam — their names, occupations, landholdings and duties — and references to coal workings, milling and fishing.

Towards the end of the 13th century the period of Scottish attacks on Northumberland began. In 1297 the year after the destruction of Hexham Priory, Wylam was 'laid waste' by the Scots under the command of William Wallace. Raids continued into the 14th century, and during one of these raids the Prior's House was destroyed and lay in ruins until it was rebuilt by the active Prior Whethamstead c. 1405. Fragments of this early medieval house, which came to be known as the Sporting House, from its use by the Prior and monks for hunting and recreation are incorporated in Wylam Hall. When Henry VIII began the suppression of the monasteries as part of the Reformation, between 1536-39, the period of 450 years during which Wylam had been in the possession of the Priors of Tynemouth came to an abrupt end.

If 1539 were the most significant landmark in Wylam's history during the 16th century, then 1679 was the local landmark in the 17th century when much of the land and property in the village was acquired by John Blackett of Horton Grange, near Ponteland; so beginning an unbroken period of almost 300 years until 1971, during which the Blackett family were Squires of Wylam.

Little information on the size of the village exists prior to the official Government censuses which commenced in 1801 — but two returns survive of those obliged to pay the Hearth Tax shortly before the Blacketts came to Wylam. In 1664, 9 people paid tax on property with one hearth and 14 are recorded as too poor to pay. In 1675, 3 paid on property with two hearths, 5 with one hearth and 17 were too poor to pay. The earliest maps of the village to survive are from 1766 and 1770, both commissioned to show the extent of land and property owned by the Blacketts and one giving information about the state of the colliery. The collieries had been important in Wylam's economy for centuries and during the mid 18th century the construction of the Wylam waggonway, one of the first in the North East, enabled coal to be transported between the colliery and staithes on the Tyne at Lemington, and thence via keels to sea-going vessels at the mouth of the Tyne for export to London and elsewhere.

The last quarter of the 18th century saw the births locally of four individuals who were to become among the world's most famous railway pioneers — William Hedley (1779), George Stephenson (1781), Timothy Hackworth (1786) and Nicholas Wood (1795). But it was after the arrival of Christopher Blackett as Squire of Wylam in 1800, that the village became of world-wide significance in the development of the steam locomotive as a means of traction. By 1815 one or two locomotives such as that illustrated on the cover of this book were hauling waggons back and forth along the 5 mile Wylam waggonway. The diversification of Wylam's industries had begun in a modest way in 1799 with the establishment by Locke, Blackett and Co. of an ingenious small lead-shot manufactory — using a disused mine-shaft, instead of building a tall shot-tower, but it was not until 1836 that a significant new industry — an ironworks — was founded. 1835/36 was remarkable for the opening of the first section of the Newcastle and Carlisle Railway between Blaydon and Hexham, along the south side of the Tyne; the development of Wylam Ironworks on the north side, and the construction by public subscription of the first bridge across the river, linking the ironworks and railway. One entrepreneur, Benjamin Thompson was the key figure associated with all three projects which were of major significance for Wylam. His two sons ran the ironworks manufacturing locomotives for various local railway and colliery companies, until the 1840s; they were succeeded by Bell Brothers, a firm who later moved to Teesside.

As a result of Wylam's industrial expansion, the population grew quite significantly during the first half of the 19th century from 673 in 1801, to 887 in 1831 and 1091 in 1851. From 1847-1856, J F B Blackett served as village squire — one of the best educated and the most caring, who also became briefly an MP for Newcastle. During his time the new British School was built (1854) and the village Reading Institute and News Room opened (1850). By the 1860s local industries were in decline with the closure of the ironworks in 1864 and of the main colliery, the Haugh Pit in 1868. Although the loss of local employment resulted in a fall in population of almost 30% between 1861 and 1871, the decline could have resulted in more serious unemployment had the closure of the Haugh Pit not coincided with the opening of the West Wylam Colliery, a mile west of Wylam, where many miners and their families moved to live and work.

In the early 1870s following the rundown of local industries the village must have given a depressing appearance. Coincidentally, as part of a campaign to improve the conditions of miners and their families, the editor of the Newcastle Weekly Chronicle published a series of reports describing each of the pit villages in Northumberland and Durham. The description of Wylam, in the issue of 17 January 1874, was highly critical. However even if the pitmen's cottages were as squalid as was claimed, investment was being made elsewhere in the village during the 1870s. A new public railway was constructed on the north side of the river between Scotswood, Newburn and Wylam following the route of the former Wylam waggonway for much of its length, and linking with the Newcastle and Carlisle Railway at Scotswood to the east and Hagg Bank, just beyond Wylam to the west. North Wylam Station opened in 1875 and the line was completed in 1876. In the same year the Wesleyans built a new Chapel, and used their earlier Chapel of 1834 as an adjoining schoolroom. A few years earlier, in 1871, village miller Edward Milburn had been busy modernising his premises, converting it from water-power to steam-power.

Although pits at Wylam Hills (behind the farm), North Wylam (near the Rift) and at the Hagg continued to work periodically the village was no longer dominated by industry and became much more attractive as a place in which to live. By the 1880s good progress was being made in redeveloping many of the sites of the sub-standard cottages on the north side of the river and the new terraces of Ingham Row, Tyne View and West View were built near the bridge in what had been known as 'Wylam Engine' or 'Low Wylam' and in the centre of the village in 'High Wylam', Burgoyne Terrace, Laburnum Terrace and Lishman's Cottages were completed. Several attractive individual stone houses were built during the 1880s and 90s, with the pleasant stone-fronted terraces of Stephenson, Falcon and Algernon following in the period to the First World War. However, the ready availability locally of red brick has meant that that has been widely used in houses on both sides of the river, sometimes where stone might have been preferable.

Thankfully stone was used for two important and prominent buildings in late Victorian times, the Parish Church of St Oswin of 1886 and the new Reading Room and Institute of 1896, both on Church Road. Similarly the Bird Inn and the Ship Inn on the Main Street were attractively re-built in stone. Although not in stone the new County Council Primary School of 1910 on Falcon Terrace, built on the site of the long-derelict ironworks was one of the early 20th Century improvements. Housing development between the wars was largely in the centre of the village along Woodcroft Road, Chapel Lane and the Main Road, and on the north side along Holeyn Hall Road and Acomb Drive. Temporary guests during the Second World War were POWs accommodated in Nissen huts on each side of Church Road above the Institute. Soon after the war the first local authority houses were built by Hexham RDC on Hedley Road, Hackworth Gardens and part of Jackson Road, and later on Bell Road and Parsons Road. More private housing followed when the former orchards at Florist Hall were developed with Woodvale Gardens and The Dene in the early 1960s. The largest development — the Dene Estate — followed in the late 1960s and 70s. These, and other smaller developments have meant that the village now has a total of some 850 dwellings and a population of almost 2,200.

Selecting photographs for this book has not been easy — some periods and subjects are well covered, but for others few if any pictures survive. I hope that those which I have chosen will be of interest — I have tried to make the captions as informative as possible within the space available. In due course perhaps it will be possible to publish a history of the village using more of the photographs available. In the meantime if any readers have old photographs of Wylam, please let me know.

Philip R B Brooks

ACKNOWLEDGEMENTS

I am most grateful to all those individuals, many of them residents of Wylam, who over the past 25 years have very kindly loaned or given me old photographs of the village; without their help this book would not have been possible. Whilst I have only been able to include a small selection of these on this occasion, they will all help to provide a valuable record of Wylam in the past, and be of interest to present and future generations.

I should also like to thank past and present staff of the Northumberland County Library and County Record Office for their help and interest over many years.

Philip R B Brooks

The following have kindly permitted photographs to be reproduced on the pages indicated:

The Science Museum (front cover), North East Water (49), Newcastle upon Tyne City Libraries and Arts (25), Northumberland County Record Office (45), H D Bowtell (27), I S Carr (28), Mrs J Efford (16), T Elliott (46).

Wylam Parish Council acknowledge with grateful thanks the support given by Northumberland County Library in the joint production of this book which has been published to celebrate the Centenary of the Parish Council.

Taken during the Centenary of George Stephenson's birth in 1881, this is the only known surviving photograph which shows the pitmen's cottages in East Water Row, alongside the bridge. Whitewashed, with red pantiled roofs they looked picturesque from a distance but in January 1874 in one of a series of critical articles about the colliery villages of Northumberland and Durham, the editor of the Newcastle Weekly Chronicle wrote a damning article about Wylam in which he described these cottages as having "two miserable rooms on the ground level, and an unceiled garret up the ladder, unfit for human habitation". They, together with the Three Tuns Inn (on the extreme right), had been demolished by the 1890s and were replaced by the much more elegant houses in Stephenson Terrace (See page 15).

By the mid 1890s when this photograph was taken, most property on the south side of the Main Street had been rebuilt and a pavement laid but the western end of the north side of the street (on the right) remained untouched. The Ship Inn, bearing the name of landlord, Henry Reay, was owned by the Blackett family. It was rebuilt to designs by local architect, William Bedlington in 1904/05 several years after Newcastle Breweries had rebuilt the neighbouring Bird Inn (See facing page). The two cottages at the end of the row have survived largely unaltered externally and are now the Wylam Tea Shop. The gable wall in the distance marks the end of a group of buildings which included the old Reading Institute (See page 34). After their demolition in the early 1920s part of the site became the small public garden known as 'Charlies Corner', named after Charles Atkinson (See page 31) who gave the garden to the village.

A quiet but muddy Main Street c. 1905. Not a vehicle in sight and so peaceful that a dog could pose in the middle of the street. Most of the buildings remain largely unchanged today. The branch of Barclays Bank and the Co-op store were built in 1915 on the corner of Chapel Lane, behind the stone wall (extreme left). Laburnum Terrace and Lishman's Cottages on the left were built in 1885 and 1882, and Burgoyne Terrace in the middle distance in 1888. The oldest building in this photograph is Laburnum House, with its blank gable wall, which is 18th century and possibly earlier. The elegant Bird Inn (right) was rebuilt by its owners, Newcastle Breweries in 1897/98. Although bearing the name of its former landlord, John Phillips, he had died by the date of this photograph and his wife Hannah succeeded him, continuing as landlady until the late 1920s.

A view of what was known in Victorian times as 'Low Wylam'. The most obvious change since this photograph was taken in about 1907 has been the redevelopment of the former corn mill (centre right behind the cart) which was burnt down in 1931 (See facing page). In the centre background are the first houses of Stephenson Terrace and right, the miller's new house (now River House) with stable and coachhouse, and the new toll house behind.Wormald House (extreme right) built by Prudhoe Colliery overman, Joseph Wormald c. 1888 incorporated a butchery business from the beginning. Thomas Leathard (whose picture appears on page 38) was village butcher for many years. The property, with its small slaughterhouse, continued as the local butcher's until 1990. The houses in Ingham Row (left) date from 1891 and the row of lime trees were planted soon after. The protective tree guards served their purpose and were not removed until 1975! The trees continue to thrive.

The scene at Wylam Mill on the morning of 9 August 1931 following a disastrous fire the previous night, which destroyed the mill premises. The village had had a corn watermill for many centuries, certainly from the time when the Priors of Tynemouth owned much of the village between the 11th and 16th centuries. A condition of the lease granted to miller Edward Milburn in 1871 was that he should convert it to a steam-powered mill, within one year, and this was when the chimney was built. He also erected the mill stables, now part of Wylam Garage. The former mill house (left) had been used for offices and storage since the new miller's house (now River House) had been built in 1902/03. Following the fire all the old buildings including the prominent mill chimney, were demolished and new premises built by the owners T G Dyke and Son. They continued to use it as a mill until the death of Mr Dyke in 1948. After subsequent use as a bottling plant and then a bakery it was converted into flats in 1984.

A thriving local 'cottage-industry' was the production of baskets made from willows gathered on the riverside. Many of the baskets produced were corves, used extensively in the local collieries to carry coal. Dating from c. 1890 this photograph shows retired miner Jack Blackburn who produced many such baskets, seated in front of the range in his cottage next to the former Wylam Brewery. The brewery occupied small premises off Ovingham Road, behind Brewery House, where Blackett Court now stands. Three inns in the village were tied to the brewery, the Ship, the Fox and Hounds and the Three Tuns (which stood on Stephenson Terrace) as well as the Glass House Inn at Lemington. The brewery closed in the late 1870s, the last maltster being George Bedlington of Ovingham. Taken by Arthur Atkinson (brother of Charles and Jennie, see page 31) this is said to be one of the first indoor flashlight pictures taken in Wylam.

When the river bridge was completed in 1836 the original toll-house was built at the southern end, across the entrance to what is now the station car park. This was replaced in 1899 when the Wylam Bridge Company erected the new toll-house shown here, at the northern end. Pedestrians were charged one penny to cross the bridge and resentment was felt by many since the wealthier inhabitants of the larger houses of South Wylam were entitled to free passes because of an agreement made between the landowner and the Bridge Company at the time the bridge was constructed. This 1906 photograph shows the toll-keeper, Edward Waugh with Gwen Waller and her brother Jack in their mail cart. The Waller family lived at 'Rushmere', Elm Bank Road between 1902 and 1920 when they left Wylam. Gwen and her sister Janet kindly gave several of the photographs which appear in this book, some of which were taken by their father, Thomas.

Not often the subject of a 'team' photograph — but this group of workmen (complete with dog) employed by builder William Strachan pose proudly in front of 24 Stephenson Terrace, which they were constructing, on 20 September 1905. Strachan was a Haltwhistle-based builder who built houses in several villages along the Tyne Valley. Within Wylam many of the houses in Wylam Wood Road, Elm Bank and the Crescent (See page 47), as well as Stephenson Terrace, were built by him. Construction of the terrace took several years to complete — commencing at each end, with the houses in the middle being the last to be completed. How welcome to have the location, date and subject of the photograph recorded on the picture itself!

The riverbank below Stephenson Terrace looks quite barren in this picture from the early 1920s; today trees growing on each side of the river obscure this view of the bridge and the terrace behind. When the bridge was built in 1836 its prime purpose was to provide a rail link from the ironworks (also opened in 1836) and the colliery, both on the north side of the river, to the newly completed railway on the south side. However a condition of the lease required that the bridge should also incorporate a roadway for 'horses, cattle, carriages and footpassengers'. The rails across the bridge were removed and the original timber decking replaced with a steel superstructure in the late 1890s, when a new Bridge Company was formed and the present toll-house built. Of special interest in this photograph is North Wylam Colliery (seen on the right) within what is now Bythorne Farm. Views showing the winding-gear of this colliery are extremely rare (See page 43).

Resentment at having to pay tolls to cross Wylam Bridge when the majority of bridges in the county were free resulted in protests to the Parish Council over many years — and in turn the Parish Council tried to exert pressure on the County Council and the Ministry of Transport to take action. Eventually after prolonged agitation by the village and protracted negotiations with the Bridge Company the County Council acquired the bridge, tollhouse and part of the access road for a total cost of £7,249, half of which was paid by the Ministry of Transport. It had previously been agreed that the Parish Council would arrange a suitable ceremony to celebrate the formal freeing of tolls and this photograph records that event on 2 December 1936 with Mrs Whitelaw, the wife of local County Councillor Robert R Whitelaw about to cut the ribbon. The gentleman not wearing a hat is County Alderman R Brogden, Chairman of the County Highways Committee and between him and Mrs Whitelaw is Richard Taylor, one of the main activists in the campaign to abolish bridge-tolls.

The unveiling of Wylam's elegant war memorial on 10 March 1923 was a sombre occasion. Much of the village attended the ceremony, performed by the 23 year old squire C J W Blackett. Among the many residents present was Sir Charles Parsons the turbine engineer who lived at Holeyn Hall (see page 30), and whose only son Major Algernon Parsons had been killed near Ypres in 1918. The selection of a suitable site for the memorial had caused much debate within the village after the war; the Parish Council and most residents wanted the attractive site on which it now stands at the bridge end, but the then Squire, Col E U Blackett, who owned the site was reluctant to agree. Fate intervened — in 1920 he died — and one of the first acts of his son Christopher, on inheriting the estate on his 21st birthday in 1921, was to accede to the wishes of local people, by giving the site for the memorial. The bridge toll-house lies in the background.

Taken in 1895, this is the only photograph so far discovered which shows the houses in the Square (extreme right). Built in the 1830s for workers at the newly established ironworks they were demolished in 1898. Twenty two houses were replaced by two. A new cottage for the toll-keeper was built by the Bridge Company in 1899 on the corner by the bridge and three years later a large new house (River House) was constructed by the miller, Edward Young. The houses in Tyne View, in the centre of the picture were built in 1887 by John Phillips, the publican at the Bird Inn, and continued to be rented-out until the 1980s. Those in West View (left) were also built to let, these by local market gardener, Matthew Maughan in 1893. Both these terraces replaced substandard pitmen's cottages. The little arched bridge in the foreground spans the old ford road — the point at which the river was crossed prior to Wylam Bridge being built in 1836. The mill chimney stands as a prominent landmark.

A panoramic view of the village from south of the river early this century. The few substantial late-Victorian stone-built houses on the left stand alone at the west end of what later became Woodcroft Road. Several sheep and cattle graze in the fields on each side of Chapel Lane which were gradually developed during the 1920s and 30s, but at this date the Black Bull Inn (extreme right) still looks across open fields. The dense copse of trees camouflages the site of Wylam Colliery (Haugh Pit) which had closed almost 40 years earlier (see page 42). The field lying between the railway cutting which crosses the centre of the scene, and the river, had been a patchwork of pitmen's gardens when the colliery was in production. Today it is the village playing field. Nets drying on the riverbank below the wood are a reminder that salmon fishing using a boat and nets, was a popular occupation in the past.

Wylam Station staff, with members of the stationmaster's family posing for this photograph c. 1885. Thomas Bell Wright, the distinguished looking stationmaster, with his flowing beard is prominent in the centre of the group, while his wife and mother stand in the background by the station house. Four of the Wrights' children disport themselves on the trolley. When Thomas Wright became stationmaster in 1873 at the age of 23, the station house which had been built when the Newcastle and Carlisle Railway was opened in 1835, had only limited accommodation. During the Wrights' occupation the North Eastern Railway added extra first floor rooms to the house to accommodate their growing family of six children. Sadly his wife Sarah died within a few years of this photograph being taken, but he continued to serve as stationmaster for a total of 39 years, until his death in 1912.

One of several posed photographs of Wylam taken in Edwardian times for W H Smith & Sons, who sold them as postcards through their network of station bookstalls. Were the smart schoolboy — or the elegantly dressed young ladies and their dog, Wylam residents — or models brought in for the photographer? The station was on the first section of the Newcastle and Carlisle Railway which opened between Blaydon and Hexham in March 1835. The distinctive North Eastern Railway over-track signal box is one of relatively few of this design remaining. The goods sidings ceased to be used in 1965 and the station car park now occupies the site. Sadly the old gas lamps and other historic features were removed in one of British Rail's modernisation programmes. The station is now one of the oldest in the world still in regular use by passengers.

The occasion of the Centenary of George Stephenson's birth in 1881 prompted at least one Newcastle photographer to take several photographs in Wylam. P M Laws who had a studio in Blackett Street took this interior view of High Street House which shows the room in which the Stephenson family lived and where George was born on 9 June 1781, as it was 100 years later. By the time that they left Wylam in 1789 the family had grown to seven — parents Robert and Mabel with their five children all occupying this single room. The National Trust, who now own the cottage, have attempted to furnish the room in a style more typical of the late 18th century when the Stephensons lived there.

Nobody suggested to the tenant of George Stephenson's birthplace that she should remove the washing draped along the fence, before the photographer took a picture of the newly renovated cottage. Photographs taken in 1881 at the time of the Stephenson Centenary show it as being in need of repair, but by 1905 when this picture was taken, repointing, construction of new chimneys and roof repairs had all been completed. The cottage dates from about 1750 and its external appearance has remained largely unchanged except for a lean-to extension at the back, added in Victorian times. The Wylam Waggonway which passed close to the front of the cottage is thought to have been constructed a few years earlier. When the Stephenson family occupied the cottage, they lived in a downstairs room, to the left of the doorway (See facing page).

North Wylam Station shortly after the turn of the century. One of the posters refers to the erection of a national memorial to Queen Victoria who died in 1901, and this probably dates the photograph at 1902/03. The group of staff includes the station master, Edwin Stabler (third from left). After the closure of Wylam Colliery in 1868 and the subsequent deterioration of the Wylam waggonway, a scheme to build a standard-gauge public railway following the route of the waggonway for much of its length between Scotswood and Wylam, and linking to the Newcastle and Carlisle line at each end, was promoted by a group of Tyneside industrialists and businessmen. The first section of the Scotswood, Newburn and Wylam Railway opened between Scotswood and Newburn on 12 July 1875 and as a single track to Wylam on 13 May 1876; the line was completed later that year. It enjoyed a brief moment of glory during the Centenary of George Stephenson's birth in 1881, but was never a financial success.

The only significant engineering structure on the Scotswood, Newburn and Wylam Railway is the distinctive bridge which carried the railway over the River Tyne at 'The Hagg' west of Wylam. The single-span, 240 foot long wrought iron bridge, with suspended roadway cost £16,000 to build and was designed by W G Laws, who later became City Engineer of Newcastle. The platform of the bridge is just three feet above the height to which the Tyne had risen in a tremendous flood in 1771. It was designed as a single span to avoid the need to construct piers in the river bed as it was feared that boring and construction works might penetrate the shallow underground workings of the local collieries which extended under the river and cause flooding. The bridge contractor was W E Jackson and Co of Newcastle, and Hawks and Crawshay of Gateshead supplied the ironwork. The bridge opened to traffic on 6 October 1876. Today it is preserved as an elegant footbridge.

The staff at North Wylam Station were clearly enthusiastic gardeners, with time to spend maintaining the station gardens in the years just before the First World War. In the background the new County Council Primary School had only just been completed (1910) by E Henderson and Son of Ponteland at a cost of less than £3,500. Before the school was built disused coke ovens and workshop buildings had remained on the site for nearly 50 years since the iron-works which formerly occupied this site closed. The single blast furnace had once stood where the roadway was later constructed. The new houses in Falcon Terrace, built by Henry Wallace & Sons of Hexham, were started late in 1906 and most were completed by 1912.

A peaceful scene at North Wylam Station on 19 July 1945 — a few weeks after VE Day. LNER locomotive 1795 G5 on the up-train for Newcastle Central, with an elderly carriage and goods van, waiting for the engine crew strolling to rejoin their charge. Coal wagons wait in the station yard siding, having delivered domestic coal. The North Wylam line, originally the Scotswood, Newburn and Wylam Railway finally closed to all traffic on 11 March 1968 although the rails were not lifted until April 1972. The disused line was subsequently acquired by Northumberland County Council and reclaimed to create a Country Park and walkway. The former station and goods yard was cleared of derelict buildings and is now a landscaped car park, with a pleasant walkway extending from Hagg Bank along to Newburn. The only feature in this photograph which remains largely unchanged is the former Stephenson's Arms Inn whose gable and chimney can just be seen above the carriage.

The elegant locomotive designed by one famous railway engineer passing the humble birthplace of another. Sir Nigel Gresley's Class A4 Pacific locomotive No 60019 'Bittern' steaming past George Stephenson's birthplace on the North Wylam line as it makes for Edinburgh via Carlisle on 12 November 1966 carrying members of the A4 Preservation Society on a Waverley railtour from Leeds. Traffic was diverted from the Newcastle and Carlisle line onto the North Wylam line for several months following the failure of the river retaining wall at Wylam Scars west of Wylam station. 'Bittern' was built by the LNER at Doncaster in 1937 and has been restored as LNER 2509 "Silver Link".

During the First World War a hospital supply depot was established in Wylam by Mrs Stirling Newall (in the centre of this picture — with black bow) who lived at Castle Hill. She organised a group of local ladies to make gauze dressings, bandages and garments for use by the troops. This photograph shows them outside the front entrance of Castle Hill. The house was designed and built in 1878 by architect Archibald M Dunn, son of Matthias Dunn, one of the first Government Inspectors of Mines for the North of England. A staunch Catholic, he designed many Catholic churches and schools on Tyneside. He and his family lived at Castle Hill until about 1900 when it was sold to F Stirling Newall. After the death of Mrs Stirling Newall in 1933 her sons gave the house to the Royal Victoria Infirmary in Newcastle and it continues in use as a hospital.

The flag hanging from the balustrade (right) and the group of soldiers gathered by the main window show Holeyn Hall in use as a Convalescent Hospital for wounded soldiers during the First World War. Holeyn Hall was built for Edward James, a Tyneside lead merchant, between 1850-53. Although the identity of the original architect is unknown, prominent Newcastle architect John Dobson was involved in designing additions or alterations to the south front in 1858. James also built the attractive stone cottages around his estate, the stable block and the fine boundary wall to the park along the road leading down to Wylam. The James family moved to Swarland Hall in 1876 and Lt. Col. M C Woods a Newcastle banker purchased the estate. Holeyn Hall's most famous resident came when (Sir) Charles Parsons the turbine engineer, acquired the property in 1894. He used workshops behind the stable block for various experiments during his ownership, which lasted until his death in 1931.

Popular figures in community life in Wylam in the first half of the century were Charles and Jennie Atkinson, seen here standing alongside a charabanc full of troops outside their home, West House, Ovingham Road c. 1918. Two of the eight children of Dr John I Atkinson and his wife Hannah, they were active in public service and charitable work locally for many years. Their father had been village doctor from 1839 until his death in 1883. Their large detached garden, on the south side of Ovingham Road was often used for fetes, garden parties and similar events (See page 39). These soldiers and nurses were from Holeyn Hall which was used as a Convalescent Hospital during the First World War (See facing page). Incidentally can anyone identify the make of the charabanc?

Almost certainly the last photograph taken before the pupils of the former British School on Woodcroft Road (right) moved into the new Primary School built by the County Council on Falcon Terrace, on 14 November 1910. Although the building in the centre had become the master's house when the British School was completed in 1854, it had itself previously served as the village school several years earlier. Much of the impetus for building the new school in 1854 came from J F B Blackett, one of the most gifted and enlightened members of the family who were Squires of Wylam for almost 300 years until 1971. Sadly he was Squire for only 9 years, dying in 1856 at the early age of 35. Remarkably little in this picture has changed — a hedge now obscures the ground floor of the former schoolhouse, which has lost its central chimney, but gained two extra windows on the first floor; the other buildings remain largely unaltered.

A scene of patriotic fervour at Wylam School. Pupils dressed in their best outfits and waving rather unwieldy flags, gather in the school playground almost certainly to celebrate Armistice Day, 11 November 1918, marking the end of the First World War. The only adult in the picture appears to be Ralph Brady (right) who served as headmaster for almost 37 years, from October 1884 until August 1921; he oversaw the move from the old school on Woodcroft Road to the new County Council school on Falcon Terrace in 1910. Natives of Morpeth, Ralph Brady and his wife Ellen, who also taught at the school for a number of years, raised a family of eight children.

Although the sign over the door of this building still claims it to be Wylam Reading Institute, its days for that purpose were numbered when this photograph was taken in the 1890s. The roof of the new (present) 'Reading Institution and Community Centre' opened in 1896 (See facing page) can be seen behind the poplar trees on the right. The Wylam Reading Institution and News Room had been founded in 1850 following a suggestion and encouragement from J F B Blackett, the village squire. The first annual report of 1850/51 lists more than 70 members, many of whom worked at the colliery. George Thompson, the local schoolmaster acted as secretary and librarian, and members paid a weekly contribution of one penny in advance. The old Institute occupied the left half of this converted cottage which stood on what is now the public garden known as 'Charlies Corner'. It was demolished in the early 1920s.

The change in character which Wylam experienced in late Victorian times resulted in the provision of various new or improved facilities. Replacement of the old Reading Institute (see facing page) became a necessity. A vacant site was acquired just below the new Parish Church of St. Oswin (left) and plans were prepared for a new Reading Room, hall and caretaker's house by local architect William Bedlington. Building commenced in 1895 and the new premises were completed and opened on 11 April the following year. The Institute President was Tyneside lead merchant Norman Cookson, who lived at Oakwood House Wylam, and he contributed generously towards the total cost of £2,600. The exterior of the Institute has remained largely unchanged in the 100 years since it was built. This photograph shows it in the 1930s.

Commemorating an important event in Wylam's history — the laying of the foundation stone for the Parish Church on 1 January 1885. Wylam was part of the parish of Ovingham, and the ancient parish church was in the smaller neighbouring village of Ovingham. The growth of Wylam during the 19th century and the fact that the Wesleyans had built a new chapel in 1876, prompted the local Anglicans to act. In 1884 they launched a campaign to raise funds to build a tin mission-church. By chance — or divine intervention — Richard or Emily Clayton of Wylam Hall met George Hedley (one of the sons of locomotive pioneer William Hedley) who had been born in Wylam in 1809 and was a staunch churchman and wealthy Durham coal owner. He promised to build a fine church for the village in memory of his parents. Newcastle architect, Robert Johnson was commissioned to prepare a design. In this photograph Richard and Emily Clayton are immediately behind the foundation stone, and George and William Hedley are in top hats, on the right. The completed church can be seen in the photograph on page 35.

Wylam's 'Wedding of the Year' 1920 took place at St Oswin's on 20 April when 25 year old Sylvia Newall, daughter of prosperous Tyneside industrialist F Stirling Newall of Castle Hill, Wylam, married 21 year old Gordon Ferguson, a chemical manufacturer of Buxton, Derbyshire. It looks as though most of the village attended — or at least came to see the bride and groom. On the left are two prominent figures in village life for 50 years, Dr William H Bishop and his sister, Alice. Dr Bishop started his practice in 1895, with the help of his sister, a trained nurse. In 1920 they moved into 'Riversdale' on Woodcroft Road which is still the surgery of the successor practice. Purchasing a car in 1904, Dr Bishop was among the first motorists in Wylam and many local children enjoyed trips in his car visiting patients in hospitals in Newcastle or in local villages. A devout Christian and founder-member of the Wylam Assembly he continued in practice until his death in 1945 aged 78.

Members of Wylam Wesleyan Chapel choir and friends display a fine selection of Edwardian fashions on an outing to one of the Yorkshire abbeys. Everyone is wearing a hat — with some splendid creations by the ladies. Most men are sporting straw boaters and the few caps look somewhat inappropriate. Chapel choirmaster and village butcher, Thomas Leathard (see page 10) has pride of place in the front row on this occasion — the minister is banished to the right hand side. Thomas Leathard's daughter, Clara is seated on his left, with his young son, Arnold, kneeling (but sensibly protecting his trousers!) in the foreground.

Another of the attractive photographs given by the Misses Gwen and Janet Waller, and thought to have been taken by their father (see page 13). However, no member of their family appears in the photograph which dates from c. 1908, and is taken in the detached garden of the Atkinsons' home, West House, Ovingham Road (See page 31). Whilst none of the individuals has yet been identified, it seems such a fine picture with the young maypole dancers and their audience all in elegant Edwardian dress that it surely merits inclusion. Perhaps someone, somewhere can provide more information about the occasion — and identify some of those taking part?

This view shows the south front of Wylam Hall as it was shortly before the Clayton Atkinson family left in 1874. A prominent naturalist and Tyneside industrialist George Clayton Atkinson leased the Hall from the Blackett family in 1853 after the previous tenant, lead merchant Edward James, had completed his new house at Holeyn Hall (see page 30) and moved out. In this photograph the main body of the Hall, with its projecting southerly wing, appears much as it does in an engraving by Ralph Bielby commissioned by John Blackett in 1770. Parts of the Hall date back to medieval times, perhaps to 1405 when Prior Whethamstead of Tynemouth rebuilt what was then the Monks 'Sporting House' following its destruction in a raid by the Scots, a century earlier. The group on the right includes members of the Clayton Atkinson family.

A different view of Wylam Hall from that on the previous page, taken in 1900 after banker Richard Clayton and his family had lived there for 25 years. When the Claytons took on a new 21 year lease of the Hall and grounds in 1891 at £240-10-0 p a they also agreed to undertake improvements to the property at a cost of at least £1,500. This included building the major extension to the Hall on the west side (left) and an entrance lodge (since demolished). The Clayton family remained at the Hall until 1909 although Richard died in 1903. Col E U Blackett added a new wing at the rear of the Hall in 1913 but the property remained largely unoccupied until the early 1920s. It was sold in 1963 but whilst being converted into flats the following year a major fire destroyed the old southern wing. None of the buildings on the right of this view survives.

Wylam's main colliery, the Haugh Pit, photographed at the time of its closure. The sloping fields in the background are those of South Wylam, developed with houses in late Victorian and Edwardian times. The colliery was situated close to the river, between what is now the village playing field and the allotments on the low riverside land — 'the haughs'. The raised storage yard on the right is now covered with mature trees. The winding engine house and chimney stood on the north side of the track which leads down to the allotments. The colliery workings extended under the river and flooding of the workings was a constant problem. Lack of investment in replacing equipment contributed to the eventual closure of the colliery by the owner, Captain E A Blackett in 1868. During the 1840s it had employed more than 200 men and boys.

The last working pit within the village itself was at North Wylam Colliery located east of Stephenson Terrace (See page 15), within what is now Bythorne Farm, but although it remained open until the early 1930s, photographs of it are very rare. This picture taken in 1921 shows Mr Bert Mills (left) the colliery blacksmith who sank the last shaft at this pit, together with Mr Ned Foggin, the colliery joiner and handyman, standing outside the smith's shop at the colliery. The National Union of Miners branch at North Wylam closed on August 21,1933.

Jack Henderson (centre with horseshoe) and his two sons, John (left) and Stanley (right) were the last blacksmiths in the village. His father Ralph Henderson had moved his family to Wylam from Byker in 1879 to set up as village blacksmith, probably succeeding George Cowens who had been local blacksmith for forty years. Jack followed his father's trade and his two sons continued the family tradition, although by the 1930s they were described as motor engineers and later undertook electrical work and much else besides. Their business started in the old forge which still survives and is thought to have originally been where the historic Wylam Colliery locomotives were built or maintained. The business subsequently expanded into the former mill-stables and adjoining premises, now occupied by Wylam Garage. This photograph was taken outside the forge in the early 1920s. Those in the back row are (left to right) Willie Lishman, Billy Caudle, Robert Milburn and George Wild.

Oliver Brothers steam wagons were a common sight on roads around Wylam in the 1920s hauling coal and roadstone. Robert Oliver lived at 'Rushmere', Elm Bank Road, with his garage and depot located in the field off Blue Bell Lane — popularly known for many years as 'Oliver's Field', but developed with houses in 1993 and now named Denecroft. This photograph c. 1925 shows Robert Oliver shortly after taking delivery of a new Super Sentinel under-type steam wagon. Each of Oliver's wagons was personalised — this one, No 5, was named 'The Wylam Rocket' and had an official carrying capacity of 6 tons but often carried loads of double that weight! Legislation introduced in Road Traffic Acts of 1930 and 1933 meant that steam wagons were no longer able to compete economically with petrol-driven lorries and their numbers diminished during the late 1930s.

Haymaking at Wylam Wood Farm - probably in the early 1920s. For many years this farm had been part of the Bradley Hall Estate, owned by the Simpson family. In 1844 it passed to the Liddells of Ravensworth. They sold the estate c. 1857 to John Walker of Seaton Burn House, who immediately leased the 139 acre Wylam Wood Farm to William Simpson of Gosforth High House. Captain E A Blackett owned it briefly during the 1860s but by 1869 it was in the ownership of C J Cruddas. In May of that year John Richardson took a 21 year lease at £310 p. a. but only remained for a short time, and several other farm tenants came and went before the Hunter family arrived in 1885. When the 1891 Census was taken the farmer was William Hunter a 35 year old widower with three young children, and his brother George also living in the farmhouse. At this time housing development began in the north-east corner of the farm (See facing page). The Hunter family remained as farm tenants until the Second World War with daughter Mildred continuing after her father died. It is thought that this picture includes members of the Hunter family.

Had it been taken fifteen years earlier, instead of in 1905, this scene at Wylam Wood Farm, South Wylam would have been of open fields not houses. The farm had been part of the Bradley Hall Estate until the 1850s and was later acquired by C J Cruddas who initiated the development of part of the farmland for housing. Whilst several houses were architect-designed and purpose-built for individual clients, others were built in groups by William Strachan a Haltwhistle builder (See page 14) who constructed many houses in South Wylam. Work on the houses in Wylam Wood Road (foreground) and the Crescent (background) started in 1902. The two short terraces (centre) were completed by the end of 1903 — a further terrace to the right, and not started in this photograph, by 1906. The detached house 'Mornington' (left) was finished early in 1904, complete with a 'coach-house, stable and saddle-room'. Houses on the remaining plots were gradually constructed in the years before 1914.

Bradley Mill in 1905. The date when the first mill was built on this site on the Stanley burn has not been established. The mill and small adjoining Bradley Mill Farm formed part of the Bradley Hall estate and in January 1857, John Walker of Seaton Burn House who had recently purchased the estate from the Liddell family of Ravensworth, leased the farm and water cornmill to Robert Marshall, a Hexham-born miller, for £60 p.a. Marshall continued as a miller/flour dealer until the 1890s. The mill buildings seen here subsequently fell into disuse and were demolished in 1931. Some of the salvaged stone was used to build the retaining wall of the bungalow 'Gracot' on the Main Road in Wylam. Nothing now remains of the mill.